Rembrandt's Beautiful Portraits

Biography 5th Grade
Children's Biography Books

BABY PROFESSOR
EDUCATION KIDS

Speedy Publishing LLC

40 E. Main St. #1156

Newark, DE 19711

www.speedypublishing.com

Copyright 2017

REMBRANDT VAN RIJN was one of the greatest painters of his or any age. He was a master not just of the technical materials—paint and surfaces and the play of light—but of depicting a wide range of human emotions, from the heroic to the weary. Let's find out about him!

REMBRANDT'S EARLY LIFE

Rembrandt was born in Leiden in the Netherlands in 1606. His father was a miller, and the family was not wealthy, but the family made sure Rembrandt had a good education.

REMBRANDT VAN RIJN

LEIDEN UNIVERSITY

He went to university at age 14, but soon left to study art full-time. He first studied with a local painter in Leiden for three years, and then moved to Amsterdam to study with Pieter Lastman, who was famous for his paintings of historical events. After less than a year in Amsterdam, having learned what Lastman had to teach him, Rembrandt moved back to Leiden.

In 1631, at age 25, Rembrandt moved to Amsterdam again. Three years later he married Saskia van Uylenburgh, who was related to an important art dealer in the city. This connection, along with Rembrandt's obvious skill, meant that many people began to commission him to paint their portraits.

SASKIA VAN UYLENBURGH

REMBRANDT IN HIS STUDIO

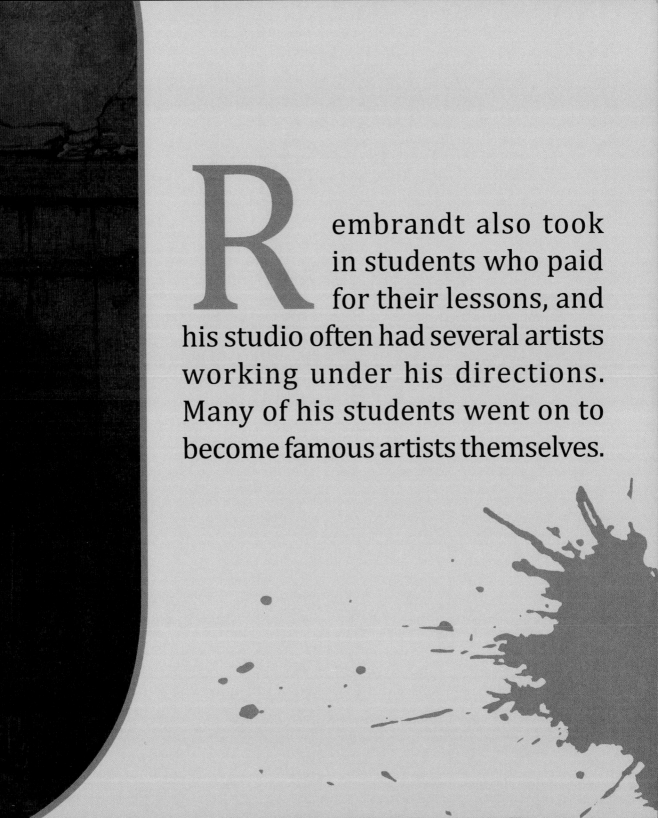

Rembrandt also took in students who paid for their lessons, and his studio often had several artists working under his directions. Many of his students went on to become famous artists themselves.

A MASTER OF ETCHING

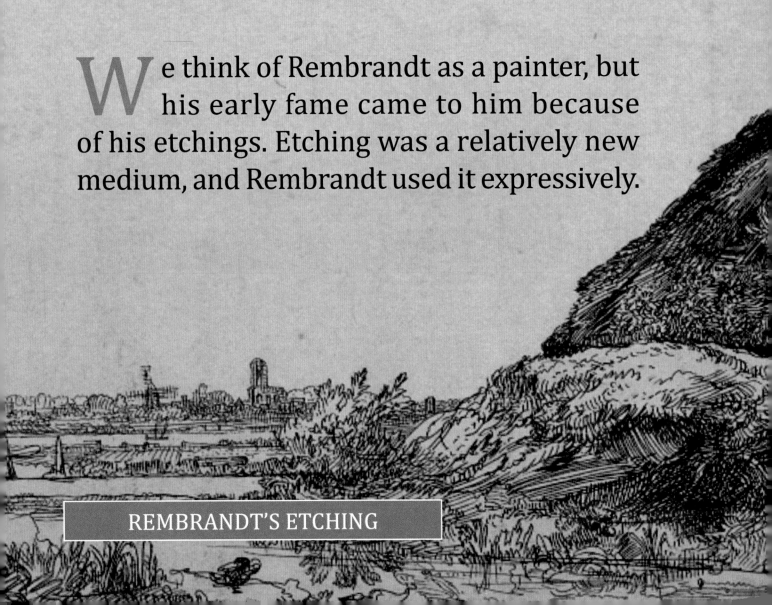

We think of Rembrandt as a painter, but his early fame came to him because of his etchings. Etching was a relatively new medium, and Rembrandt used it expressively.

REMBRANDT'S ETCHING

E tching is different from engraving or wood-cuts:

- When you make an engraving, you carve lines into a metal plate using a sharp, v-shaped tool. Then the plate is used in a printing press to make many copies of the

original. The images of people or buildings on United States dollars, for instance, were created as etchings. The lines are fine and regular and the images are precise.

- With wood cuts, you carve away everything from one surface of a block of wood except the parts that you want to print. Then you ink the wood block and apply the paper you want the print on to it. The resulting images tend to be less precise and more flowing than those from an engraving.

WOOD CUT ART

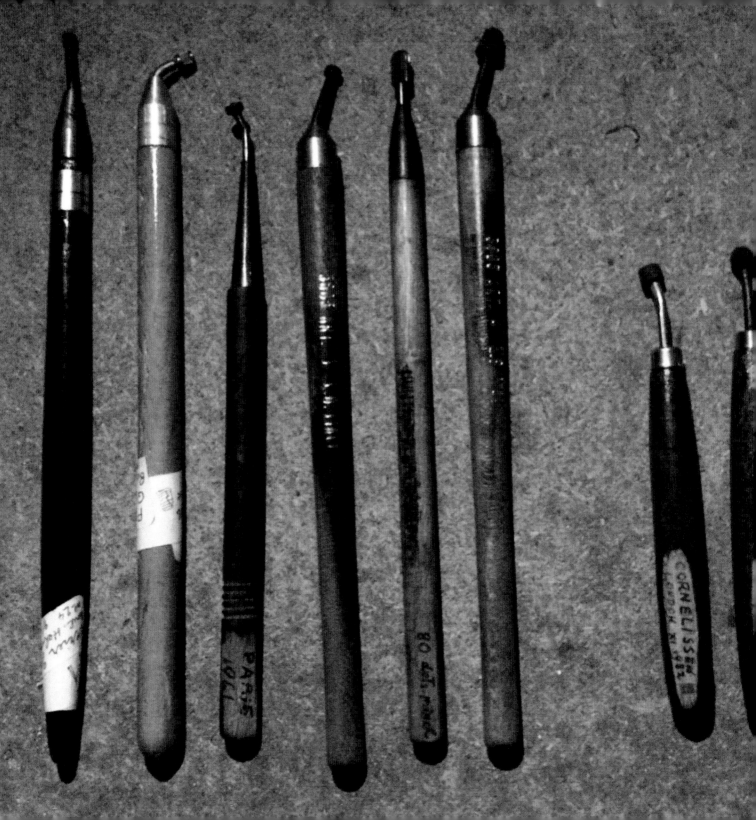

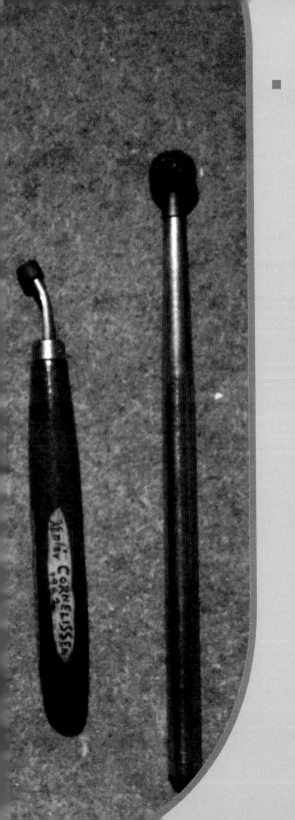

To create a plate for etching, you cover the printing plate with a thin coating of some resistant material, like resin. Then you use a thin, sharp needle to cut through the coating to, but not into, the surface of the plate. It is much easier to cut through the coating than into the plate, so the lines usually flow more smoothly and have more expressive curve than lines in an engraving.

W hen the image is done, you apply acid to it. The acid eats into the plate wherever you have removed the coating, cutting an irregular, vibrating line. Then you rinse off both the acid and the rest of the coating, and use the plate in a printing press.

REMBRANDT'S MOTHER

Rembrandt was a master of the dynamic line achieved in etching from an early age. When he was 22, he etched a portrait of his mother that captures the details of her face, the flow of her hair, and a sense of the space she is sitting in with remarkable beauty.

With all three of these methods the artist can produce many copies of the work, and Rembrandt regularly sold copies of his most popular etchings right up until his death. He made almost 300 etchings, some of them no larger than postcards, and almost 100 of his plates still exist.

REMBRANDT'S SELF PORTRAIT

REMBRANDT'S PRINTING STUDIO

PUBLIC SUCCESS, PRIVATE SORROW

Rembrandt's professional life was successful early, and he sold many paintings and prints and made a good income from teaching students. He was able to buy a house in Amsterdam in 1639, when he was 33. You can visit the house today, it is maintained as a Rembrandt museum, and shows how he lived and what his studio looked like.

At the same time Rembrandt's private life saw much sadness. He and his wife Saskia had four children between 1635 and 1641, but the three oldest died early. Only Titus, the youngest, survived to adulthood. Saskia herself died at age 30, in 1642.

THE ARTIST'S SON, TITUS

PORTRAIT OF HENDRICKJE STOFELLS

In 1649, Rembrandt hired a housekeeper, Hendrickje Stoffels, and she eventually became his common-law wife. She was also the model for many of his paintings, as Saskia had been.

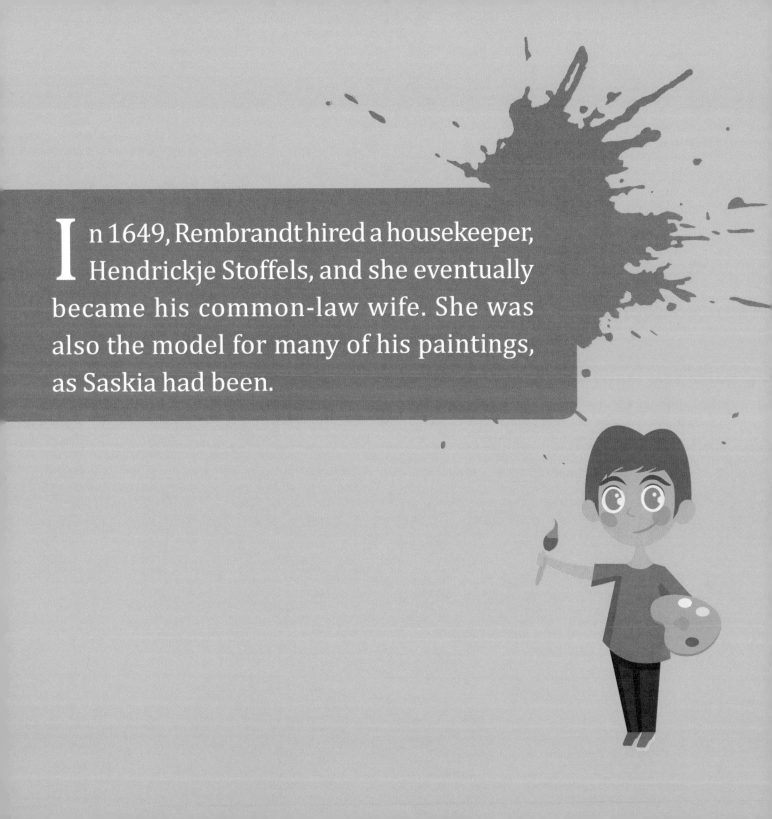

REMBRANDT'S HOUSE

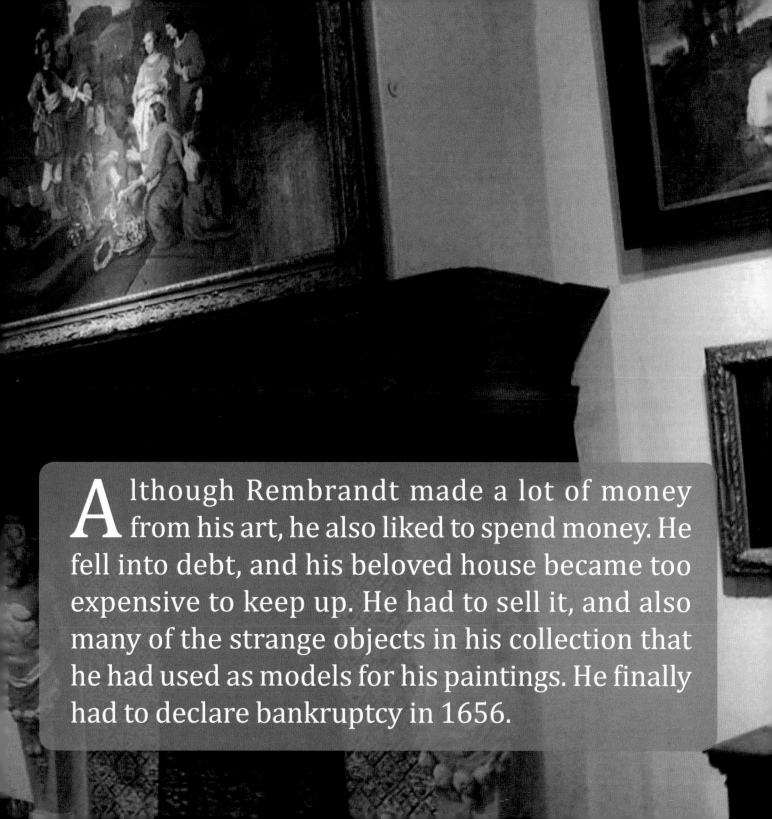

Although Rembrandt made a lot of money from his art, he also liked to spend money. He fell into debt, and his beloved house became too expensive to keep up. He had to sell it, and also many of the strange objects in his collection that he had used as models for his paintings. He finally had to declare bankruptcy in 1656.

THE JEWISH BRIDE

These private sorrows did not prevent Rembrandt from working. Some of his greatest paintings come from this period, including Bathsheba in 1654 (now in the Louvre in Paris), a self-portrait in 1658 (in the Frick Collection in the United States), and The Jewish Bride in 1665.

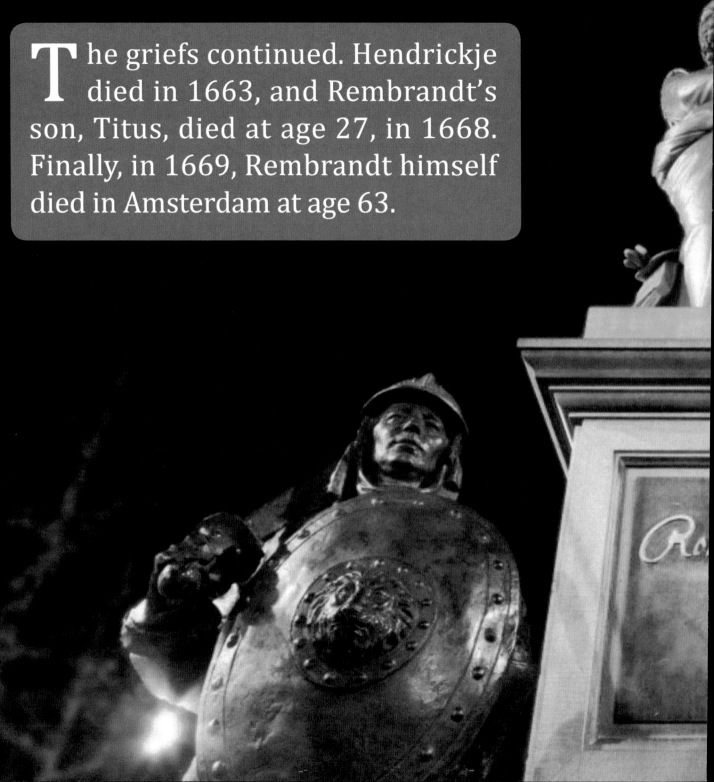

The griefs continued. Hendrickje died in 1663, and Rembrandt's son, Titus, died at age 27, in 1668. Finally, in 1669, Rembrandt himself died in Amsterdam at age 63.

REMBRANDT STATUE

REMBRANDT'S STYLE

Rembrandt's style with etchings was exciting and fresh. The figures, with their uncombed hair, tired faces, or surprised expressions, seemed caught in the act of living.

In painting, also, Rembrandt developed a style of his own. He painted his portraits with a limited palette of colors, mainly dark earth tones and golden highlights. He mastered the Italian art of "chiaroscuro", or "clear-obscure" which used a strong light source to highlight the subject of the painting and to throw the rest of the work into heavy shadows.

This created an illusion of depth around the painted figure. Rembrandt spent most of his time on the subject's head and hands, and let the body blend into the background.

THE NIGHT WATCH

One of Rembrandt's most remarkable paintings was The Night Watch, completed in 1642. He was commissioned to do a group portrait of a regiment of volunteers who helped to keep order in Amsterdam after dark—cities did not have professional police forces until the nineteenth century.

R embrandt produced a stunning work of complexity, humor, and insight into the characters of people. It is almost life-sized, and there are eighteen key figures who contributed to the cost of the painting, plus as

many "minor" figures. However, each person in the painting is lovingly depicted in action, in a complex scene that leads the eye round and round, so it is like a gallery of almost forty portraits.

Nothing like this had ever been seen before, and a lot of the men who had paid for the painting did not like it. Each one felt he should have been larger, clearer, and made more beautiful than Rembrandt painted him. Although now we see this as a wonderful success in terms of art, in its time it was a failure, and it damaged Rembrandt's reputation so he got many fewer commissions.

SELF-PORTRAITS

R embrandt used himself as his model many times. We know of more than 90 Rembrandt self-portraits, and he appears as the model in several of his etchings. We can follow his life, from exuberant youth to the challenges of adulthood, to somber old age; and at the same time we can see the remarkable effect when a great artists turns an unflinching eye on his subject.

In the story of his own life that he painted, Rembrandt lets us see him in many moods, in many lights: he hides nothing, and includes every detail that helps make the painting rich and exciting.

AN ARTIST'S LIFE

The key to Rembrandt's life as an artist was his curiosity. He wanted to find out what he could make his medium do, whether it was paint or etching plates or just chalk on a piece of paper. He wanted to see how much he could show of the inner lives of his subjects.

M ore than that, he did not just paint the rich and comfortable, the people who could afford to buy such a painting. Many of

his works are of the poor, of people broken
down by their lives, people exhausted by sleep
or even on the point of death.

REMBRANDT'S CHRIST IN THE STORM ON THE LAKE OF GALILEE

Rembrandt seems always to have been dissatisfied with what he had achieved so far, and tried to get closer with each new painting to the scene he could visualize inside his head, by experimenting with new techniques, different and original subjects, and unusual compositions. For all the risks he took with his art, it is remarkable how few of his paintings are not effective or pleasing to look at. Each experiment took him closer to what he wanted to achieve.

ACHIEVE GREAT THINGS

You don't know what you can do unless you try to do it—and stick to it to for a while, as Rembrandt did. Here are Baby Professor books about people who achieved great things, even if they were not the things they thought they were going to do with their lives: Sally Ride: The First American Woman in Space, A Rich Man in Poor Clothing: The Story of St. Francis of Assisi, and Marquis de Lafayette: The Hero of Two Worlds.